Table Of Contents

Chapter 1: The Importance of Mindfulness in Entrepreneurship

Chapter 2: Techniques for Reducing Stress in Business

Chapter 3: Mindful Time Management

Chapter 4: Mindful Communication in the Workplace

Chapter 5: Mindful Leadership

Chapter 6: Mindfulness for Parent-Entrepreneurs

Chapter 7: Mindful Self-Care for Women Entrepreneurs

Chapter 8: Mindful Entrepreneurship for Mental Wellness

Chapter 9: The Future of Mindful Entrepreneurship

Conclusion: The Power of Mindful Entrepreneurship for Mental Wellness

Chapter 1: The Importance of Mindfulness in Entrepreneurship
What is Mindfulness?

Mindfulness is a state of being aware of the present moment, without judgment or distraction. It is a way of paying attention to what is happening around us, and within us, in a non-reactive manner. Mindfulness is not just a state of mind, but also a practice that can be cultivated through various techniques such as meditation, breathing exercises, and mindful movement.

In today's fast-paced world, it is easy to get caught up in the stress and chaos of everyday life. As women, parents, and business owners, we often juggle multiple roles and responsibilities, leaving little time for self-care and reflection. Mindfulness can help us to slow down, tune in, and connect with ourselves and others in a more meaningful way.

One of the key benefits of mindfulness is its ability to reduce stress and promote mental wellness. By practicing mindfulness regularly, we can learn to manage our emotions and thoughts more effectively, and develop a greater sense of calm and clarity. This can be especially helpful in high-pressure situations such as business meetings, parenting challenges, or personal crises.

Another benefit of mindfulness is its ability to enhance our creativity and productivity. When we are fully present and engaged in the moment, we are more likely to come up with innovative ideas and solutions. Mindfulness can also help us to stay focused and avoid distractions, which can be particularly useful in today's digital age.

There are many different ways to practice mindfulness, and no one-size-fits-all approach. Some people find meditation to be a helpful tool, while others prefer to practice mindfulness through movement or creative pursuits. Whatever method you choose, it is important to approach mindfulness with an open mind and a willingness to learn.

In conclusion, mindfulness is a powerful tool for reducing stress, promoting mental wellness, and enhancing our creativity and productivity. By incorporating mindfulness practices into our daily lives, we can cultivate a greater sense of calm, clarity, and connection, which can ultimately lead to greater success and fulfillment in all areas of our lives.

The Benefits of Mindfulness for Entrepreneurs

Entrepreneurship is an exciting journey that can be full of challenges and stress. As a business owner, you often find yourself juggling multiple tasks, making important decisions, and dealing with the ups and downs of running a business. It's no surprise that stress and burnout are common among entrepreneurs, and that's where mindfulness comes in.

Mindfulness is the practice of being fully present and aware of the current moment without judgment. It's an effective tool for reducing stress, improving mental wellness, and enhancing overall well-being. Here are some of the benefits of mindfulness for entrepreneurs:

1. Reduced stress levels

Starting and running a business can be stressful, and chronic stress can have negative effects on your physical and mental health. Mindfulness practices such as meditation and deep breathing can help you manage stress and reduce its impact on your body and mind.

2. Improved focus and productivity

When you're mindful, you're better able to focus on the task at hand and avoid distractions. This can help you be more productive and efficient in your work, leading to a more successful business.

3. Better decision-making

Mindfulness can help you make better decisions by reducing the influence of emotions and biases. When you're mindful, you're able to approach situations with a clear and open mind, allowing you to make more rational and informed decisions.

4. Enhanced creativity

Mindfulness practices can stimulate creativity by quieting the mind and allowing new ideas to emerge. This can be especially beneficial for entrepreneurs who need to constantly come up with innovative ideas to keep their business thriving.

5. Improved relationships

Mindfulness can help you become a better listener and communicator, which can improve your relationships with employees, clients, and other stakeholders. By being fully present and attentive, you can build stronger connections and foster a more positive work environment.

In conclusion, mindfulness is a powerful tool that can help entrepreneurs reduce stress, improve mental wellness, and enhance overall well-being. By incorporating mindfulness practices into your daily routine, you can become a more effective and successful business owner.

The Science of Mindfulness

The Science of Mindfulness

Mindfulness has become a popular term in recent years, but what exactly is it, and how does it work? In essence, mindfulness is the practice of paying attention to the present moment, without judgment or distraction. It can involve meditation, breathing exercises, or simply being fully present in whatever activity you are engaged in.

But what does the science say about the benefits of mindfulness? Studies have shown that regular mindfulness practice can reduce stress, anxiety, and depression, and improve overall mental health. It can also improve cognitive function, including attention, memory, and decision-making.

One of the key ways that mindfulness works is by reducing activity in the default mode network (DMN) of the brain. This is the network that is active when we are not focused on any particular task, and it tends to be associated with self-referential thinking, worry, and rumination. By reducing activity in the DMN, mindfulness practice can help us break out of negative thought patterns and focus more on the present moment.

Another way that mindfulness can promote mental wellness is by increasing activity in the prefrontal cortex (PFC) of the brain. This is the part of the brain that is responsible for executive functions like decision-making, planning, and self-control. By strengthening the PFC through mindfulness practice, we can become more resilient in the face of stress and better able to regulate our emotions.

Of course, like any form of self-care, mindfulness is not a magic cure-all. It takes time and practice to develop the skills and habits that will help you reap the benefits. But with consistent effort, mindfulness can be a powerful tool for reducing stress and promoting mental wellness, both in your personal life and in your business. So why not give it a try? Start by setting aside a few minutes each day to practice mindfulness, and see how it can transform your life.

Chapter 2: Techniques for Reducing Stress in Business
The Effects of Stress on Mental Health

The Effects of Stress on Mental Health

Stress is a normal part of life, and it can be beneficial in small doses. It can help you stay focused and alert, and it can even motivate you to work harder. However, prolonged stress can have serious negative effects on your mental health, and it's important to understand these effects so you can take steps to mitigate them.

One of the most significant effects of stress on mental health is anxiety. When you're stressed, your body produces more cortisol, a hormone that can trigger feelings of anxiety. Anxiety can manifest in a variety of ways, including racing thoughts, difficulty sleeping, and physical symptoms like headaches or stomachaches.

Another common effect of stress on mental health is depression. When you're under a lot of stress, it can be difficult to find joy in the things you used to enjoy. You may feel more irritable or hopeless than usual, and you may struggle to concentrate or make decisions.

Stress can also affect your relationships with others. When you're stressed, you may be more likely to lash out at others or withdraw from social situations. This can lead to strained relationships with family members, friends, or colleagues.

Finally, stress can have physical effects on your body that can in turn affect your mental health. For example, chronic stress can lead to high blood pressure, heart disease, and other health problems that can impact your overall wellbeing. If you're not taking care of your physical health, it can be difficult to maintain good mental health as well.

Overall, it's clear that stress can have serious negative effects on your mental health. If you're a woman, parent, or business owner who is concerned about mental health self-care, it's important to take steps to reduce stress in your life. This might include practicing mindfulness techniques like meditation or yoga, setting boundaries to protect your time and energy, and seeking support from a mental health professional if needed. With the right tools and resources, you can minimize the negative effects of stress and promote mental wellness in your life and business.

Techniques for Managing Stress

Stress is an inevitable part of life, especially for women, parents, and business owners. The pressure to perform well in multiple roles can take a toll on one's mental and physical health. However, there are various techniques that can help manage stress and promote mental wellness in business. In this subchapter, we will discuss some of these techniques that can help you lead a more balanced and fulfilling life.

1. Mindfulness Meditation

Mindfulness meditation is a practice that involves focusing your attention on the present moment and accepting your thoughts and feelings without judgment. Regular practice of mindfulness meditation has been proven to reduce stress, anxiety, and depression. You can start by setting aside a few minutes each day to practice mindfulness meditation. There are many guided meditation apps available that can help you get started.

2. Exercise

Exercise is a great way to reduce stress and improve your mental and physical health. Physical activity releases endorphins, which are natural mood boosters. You can try incorporating some form of exercise into your daily routine, such as going for a walk in the morning or taking a yoga class. Find an activity that you enjoy and that fits into your schedule.

3. Time Management

Poor time management can lead to stress and burnout. It is essential to prioritize your tasks and allocate your time accordingly. Make a to-do list and schedule your day to ensure that you are not overburdened. Delegate tasks, if possible, to reduce your workload.

4. Self-Care

Self-care is essential for mental wellness. It involves taking care of yourself physically, emotionally, and mentally. Get enough sleep, eat a healthy diet, and take breaks when needed. Engage in activities that make you happy and relaxed, such as reading a book, watching a movie, or spending time with loved ones.

5. Seek Support

It is okay to ask for help when you are feeling overwhelmed. Reach out to family, friends, or a mental health professional for support. Join a support group or a community of like-minded individuals who can offer you guidance and support.

In conclusion, managing stress is crucial for mental wellness in business. These techniques can help you reduce stress and promote a healthy work-life balance. Remember to prioritize your mental and physical health, and seek support when needed. With these practices, you can lead a more mindful and fulfilling life.

Mindful Breathing Exercises

Mindful Breathing Exercises

Breathing is a natural process that we often take for granted. However, when done mindfully, breathing can be a powerful tool for promoting mental wellness and reducing stress. Mindful breathing exercises are simple techniques that can be practiced anytime, anywhere, and by anyone. In this chapter, we will explore some of the most effective mindful breathing exercises that you can incorporate into your daily routine.

1. Deep Breathing

Deep breathing is a simple yet powerful technique that can help you relax and reduce stress. Start by sitting or standing in a comfortable position, with your feet firmly planted on the ground. Take a deep breath in through your nose, filling your lungs with air. Hold your breath for a few seconds, and then exhale slowly through your mouth. Repeat this process for a few minutes, focusing on the sensation of the air moving in and out of your body.

2. Counted Breathing

Counted breathing is another effective technique that you can use to promote mental wellness and reduce stress. Start by sitting or standing in a comfortable position, with your feet firmly planted on the ground. Take a deep breath in and count to four. Hold your breath for a few seconds, and then exhale slowly while counting to four again. Repeat this process for a few minutes, focusing on the counting and the sensation of the air moving in and out of your body.

3. Box Breathing

Box breathing is a more advanced technique that can help you reduce stress and improve focus. Start by sitting or standing in a comfortable position, with your feet firmly planted on the ground. Take a deep breath in and count to four. Hold your breath for four seconds, and then exhale slowly while counting to four. Hold your breath for four seconds again, and then repeat the process. Try to maintain a steady rhythm, focusing on the sensation of the air moving in and out of your body.

Incorporating mindful breathing exercises into your daily routine can have a significant impact on your mental wellness and overall wellbeing. These simple techniques can help you reduce stress, improve focus, and promote relaxation. As a busy woman, parent, or business owner, it is essential to take care of your mental health. Mindful breathing exercises can help you do just that. So, take a deep breath, and start practicing today!

Chapter 3: Mindful Time Management
The Importance of Time Management for Mental Wellness

The Importance of Time Management for Mental Wellness

In today's fast-paced world, time is a valuable commodity that we cannot afford to waste. As women, parents, and business owners, we have numerous responsibilities that require our attention. Juggling these tasks can be overwhelming, leading to stress and anxiety. Therefore, it is crucial to manage our time effectively to maintain our mental wellness.

Time management is the process of planning, organizing, and prioritizing activities to achieve specific goals efficiently. It involves being mindful of how we allocate our time and avoiding time-wasting activities. Time management skills are essential for mental wellness as they help us to focus, reduce stress, and increase productivity.

Effective time management allows us to prioritize our responsibilities and avoid being overwhelmed by our to-do lists. By setting realistic goals and deadlines, we can create a sense of control over our lives, leading to a more positive outlook. Furthermore, time management enables us to avoid procrastination, which can lead to stress and anxiety.

One of the most significant benefits of time management is that it allows us to create time for self-care. As women, parents, and business owners, we often neglect our mental and physical needs while prioritizing our responsibilities. However, self-care is essential for mental wellness and reducing stress. By managing our time, we can create a schedule that includes time for exercise, meditation, hobbies, and spending time with loved ones.

Time management also helps us to avoid burnout, a state of emotional, physical, and mental exhaustion caused by prolonged periods of stress. Burnout can lead to depression, anxiety, and other mental health issues. By managing our time effectively, we can reduce stress levels and avoid burnout.

In conclusion, time management is crucial for mental wellness. As women, parents, and business owners, we have multiple responsibilities that require our attention. Effective time management skills help us to prioritize our tasks, avoid procrastination, create time for self-care, and reduce stress levels. By implementing time management techniques, we can improve our mental wellness and lead a more fulfilling life.

Techniques for Effective Time Management

Time management is an essential skill for business owners, parents, and women who want to achieve their goals while still taking care of their mental wellness. Effective time management is about prioritizing tasks, minimizing distractions, and focusing on what matters most.

Here are some techniques for effective time management that you can use to reduce stress and promote mental wellness in your business and personal life.

1. Prioritize tasks

The first step in effective time management is to prioritize tasks. Make a list of all the tasks you need to complete and then rank them in order of importance. Focus on completing the most important tasks first, and then move on to the less important ones.

2. Create a schedule

Creating a schedule is a great way to manage your time effectively. Set aside specific times for tasks, such as checking emails or making phone calls. This will help you stay on track and avoid getting distracted.

3. Minimize distractions

Distractions can be a major time-waster. Minimize distractions by turning off notifications on your phone, closing unnecessary tabs on your computer, and creating a quiet workspace.

4. Take breaks

Taking breaks is essential for mental wellness. Schedule regular breaks throughout the day to recharge your mind and prevent burnout.

5. Delegate tasks

Delegating tasks is a great way to save time and reduce stress. Identify tasks that can be delegated to others, such as administrative tasks or social media management. This will free up your time to focus on more important tasks.

6. Use time tracking tools

Time tracking tools can help you identify where you're spending your time and where you can make improvements. Use tools like RescueTime or Toggl to track your time and identify areas where you can be more efficient.

In conclusion, effective time management is essential for reducing stress and promoting mental wellness in business and personal life. Prioritizing tasks, creating a schedule, minimizing distractions, taking breaks, delegating tasks, and using time tracking tools are all techniques that can help you manage your time effectively. By implementing these techniques, you can achieve your goals while still taking care of your mental wellness.

Mindful Prioritization

Mindful Prioritization: The Key to Reducing Stress and Achieving Success in Business

As a woman, parent, and business owner, you are likely juggling multiple responsibilities and tasks on a daily basis. It can be overwhelming and stressful trying to balance it all, but there is a way to reduce stress and achieve success in business: mindful prioritization.

Mindful prioritization is the art of choosing what is most important and focusing your energy and attention on those tasks. It is about being intentional with your time and making sure that you are not wasting it on things that are not important or do not align with your goals.

To practice mindful prioritization, start by setting clear goals for yourself and your business. What do you want to achieve? What are your priorities? Once you have a clear understanding of your goals, you can begin to prioritize your tasks and activities accordingly.

One technique for prioritization is the Eisenhower Matrix, which categorizes tasks into four quadrants: urgent and important, important but not urgent, urgent but not important, and neither urgent nor important. By using this framework, you can identify which tasks are critical and require immediate attention, and which can be delegated or postponed.

Another technique is to break down your goals into smaller, more manageable tasks. This can help you avoid feeling overwhelmed and make progress towards your goals every day. Prioritize the most important tasks and tackle them first thing in the morning when you have the most energy and focus.

It is also important to be mindful of your own limitations and boundaries. As a business owner, it can be tempting to work around the clock and neglect your own self-care. However, this can lead to burnout and decreased productivity. Set realistic expectations for yourself and make time for activities that promote mental wellness, such as exercise, meditation, or spending time with loved ones.

In conclusion, mindful prioritization is a powerful tool for reducing stress and achieving success in business. By setting clear goals, using prioritization techniques, and being mindful of your own limitations, you can manage your time and energy effectively and achieve your goals with ease. Remember, success is not about doing everything, but about doing the right things.

Chapter 4: Mindful Communication in the Workplace
The Importance of Mindful Communication

The Importance of Mindful Communication

As women, parents and business owners, we all know the importance of communication in our daily lives. Whether it is communicating with our colleagues, partners, families or friends, communication is at the core of our interactions. However, we often overlook the impact that our communication style can have on our mental wellness and stress levels.

Mindful communication is the practice of being present and fully engaged in the act of communicating. It involves being aware of our thoughts, emotions and reactions while we are communicating, as well as being mindful of the impact our words and actions may have on others.

By practicing mindful communication, we can improve our mental wellness and reduce stress levels. Here are some key reasons why mindful communication is so important:

1. It improves relationships: Mindful communication allows us to be more present and engaged in our interactions with others. This can help to build stronger relationships, as we are better able to understand and respond to the needs of others.

2. It reduces misunderstandings: Misunderstandings can often lead to conflict and stress. By practicing mindful communication, we can better understand the perspectives of others and avoid misunderstandings.

3. It promotes empathy: Mindful communication involves being present and fully engaged in the act of listening. This can help us to develop a deeper sense of empathy for others, which can lead to more positive interactions and relationships.

4. It reduces stress: Mindful communication can help to reduce stress levels by promoting a sense of calm and clarity in our interactions with others.

To practice mindful communication, it is important to be present and fully engaged in the act of communicating. This involves being aware of our thoughts, emotions and reactions, as well as being mindful of the impact our words and actions may have on others.

In conclusion, mindful communication is a key tool for improving our mental wellness and reducing stress levels. By practicing mindful communication, we can build stronger relationships, reduce misunderstandings, promote empathy and reduce stress. As women, parents and business owners, it is important to prioritize our mental health self-care by incorporating practices that promote mental wellness and reduce stress. Mindful communication is a simple but powerful technique that we can all incorporate into our daily lives to promote our mental wellness and reduce stress levels.

Techniques for Mindful Communication

Mindful communication is a powerful tool for reducing stress and promoting mental wellness in business. It is an essential skill that can help you to communicate more effectively, build better relationships, and achieve greater success in your personal and professional life.

There are several techniques that you can use to practice mindful communication, including:

1. Active Listening

Active listening is a technique that involves focusing your attention fully on the person speaking to you. It involves being fully present in the moment, without judgment or distraction. When you practice active listening, you show the other person that you value their opinion and are interested in what they have to say.

2. Empathy

Empathy is the ability to understand and share the feelings of another person. When you practice empathy, you put yourself in the other person's shoes and try to see things from their perspective. This can help you to build stronger relationships and communicate more effectively.

3. Mindful Speaking

Mindful speaking involves being aware of how your words and tone of voice can impact others. It involves speaking in a clear and concise manner, without judgment or criticism. When you practice mindful speaking, you can communicate your message more effectively and avoid misunderstandings.

4. Nonviolent Communication

Nonviolent communication is a technique that involves expressing your needs and feelings in a way that is respectful and non-threatening. It involves using "I" statements instead of "you" statements, and focusing on the problem rather than the person. When you practice nonviolent communication, you can resolve conflicts more effectively and build stronger relationships.

5. Mindful Body Language

Body language is an important aspect of communication. When you practice mindful body language, you are aware of how your posture, facial expressions, and gestures can impact others. You can use this knowledge to communicate your message more effectively and build stronger relationships.

In conclusion, mindful communication is a powerful tool for reducing stress and promoting mental wellness in business. By practicing active listening, empathy, mindful speaking, nonviolent communication, and mindful body language, you can communicate more effectively, build better relationships, and achieve greater success in your personal and professional life.

The Benefits of Mindful Communication

The Benefits of Mindful Communication

Communication is a vital tool in business and personal relationships. However, it can be challenging to communicate effectively, especially when stress levels are high. That's where mindful communication comes in. Mindful communication is a technique that helps you listen and speak with intention and awareness. It involves being present in the moment, paying attention to your thoughts and feelings, and being empathetic towards others.

Women, parents, and business owners have a lot on their plate. The pressure to succeed in business and manage family life can be overwhelming, leading to stress and burnout. By practicing mindful communication, you can reduce stress levels and promote mental wellness. Here are some of the benefits of mindful communication:

1. Improves Relationships

Mindful communication helps you build better relationships with others. When you listen to someone with intention and empathy, you create a safe space for them to express themselves. This fosters trust and understanding, leading to stronger relationships.

2. Reduces Conflict

Miscommunication can lead to conflict, which can be detrimental to business and personal relationships. Mindful communication helps you avoid misunderstandings by listening and responding with intention. This reduces the likelihood of conflict and helps resolve issues quickly.

3. Increases Productivity

When stress levels are high, productivity can suffer. By practicing mindful communication, you can reduce stress levels and improve focus. This leads to increased productivity, which is essential for business owners and busy parents.

4. Promotes Mental Wellness

Mindful communication is a form of self-care that promotes mental wellness. When you practice mindful communication, you are present in the moment, which reduces anxiety and stress. This helps you stay calm and focused, promoting mental wellness and reducing the risk of burnout.

In conclusion, mindful communication is a powerful tool for women, parents, and business owners. By practicing mindful communication, you can improve relationships, reduce conflict, increase productivity, and promote mental wellness. Take the time to practice mindful communication in your personal and professional life, and you'll see the benefits in no time.

Chapter 5: Mindful Leadership
The Role of Mindfulness in Leadership

The Role of Mindfulness in Leadership

As a business owner, it is essential to lead with clarity, compassion, and focus. Mindfulness is a powerful tool that can help you achieve these goals and create a culture of mental wellness in your workplace.

Mindfulness is the practice of being fully present and engaged in the moment. It is about paying attention to your thoughts, feelings, and surroundings without judgment or distraction. This type of awareness can help you make better decisions, build stronger relationships with your employees and customers, and reduce stress and anxiety.

As a leader, mindfulness can help you stay calm and focused during challenging situations. It can also help you communicate more effectively with your team, leading to better collaboration and productivity. By practicing mindfulness, you can become more aware of your own biases and limitations, allowing you to make more informed and strategic decisions.

One of the key benefits of mindfulness is its ability to reduce stress and promote mental wellness. As a business owner, you are likely familiar with the high levels of stress that come with running a company. By practicing mindfulness regularly, you can learn to manage stress more effectively, reducing the negative impact it can have on your mental and physical health.

Mindfulness can also help you build stronger relationships with your employees and customers. By being fully present and engaged during conversations, you can create a sense of trust and connection that is essential for building lasting relationships. This type of connection can also help you better understand the needs and concerns of your employees and customers, allowing you to create a more inclusive and supportive workplace.

In conclusion, mindfulness is a powerful tool that can help you become a better leader and create a culture of mental wellness in your workplace. By practicing mindfulness regularly, you can reduce stress, improve decision-making, and build stronger relationships with your team and customers. As a business owner, investing in your own mental health and well-being is essential for creating a thriving and sustainable business that supports both your employees and your bottom line.

Techniques for Mindful Leadership

Techniques for Mindful Leadership

Being a business owner or a leader can be overwhelming. The constant pressure to perform, meet deadlines, and manage a team can take a toll on your mental and emotional well-being. However, with the right techniques, you can become a mindful leader who is not only successful but also mentally and emotionally healthy.

Here are some techniques for mindful leadership:

1. Practice mindfulness: Mindfulness is the practice of being present in the moment and aware of your thoughts and feelings. It can help reduce stress and anxiety, increase focus and productivity, and improve decision-making. As a leader, practicing mindfulness can help you be more present and attentive to your team, customers, and business needs.

2. Develop self-awareness: Self-awareness is the ability to recognize and understand your own emotions, thoughts, and behaviors. It can help you manage your

emotions, communicate effectively, and build better relationships. By developing self-awareness, you can become a more empathetic and compassionate leader, which can foster a positive work environment.

3. Cultivate resilience: Resilience is the ability to bounce back from setbacks and recover from stress. It can help you stay focused and motivated during challenging times. As a leader, cultivating resilience can help you lead your team through difficult situations and inspire them to stay positive and motivated.

4. Practice active listening: Active listening is the practice of fully engaging with the person speaking and understanding their perspective. It can help build trust and improve communication. As a leader, practicing active listening can help you understand your team's needs and concerns, which can lead to better decision-making and problem-solving.

5. Create a positive work environment: A positive work environment can help reduce stress and improve mental and emotional well-being. As a leader, you can create a positive work environment by promoting open communication, creating a supportive culture, and recognizing and rewarding your team's achievements.

In conclusion, being a mindful leader requires practice and dedication. By incorporating these techniques into your leadership style, you can create a more positive work environment, foster better relationships with your team, and improve your mental and emotional well-being. Remember, taking care of yourself as a leader is not only beneficial for you but also for your business and team.

The Benefits of Mindful Leadership

The Benefits of Mindful Leadership

In today's fast-paced business world, stress, anxiety and burnout are increasingly common. The pressure to succeed can take a toll on anyone, but it can be especially challenging for women who are juggling multiple roles as parents and business owners. This is where mindful leadership can make a difference.

Mindful leadership is the practice of being fully present and attentive in the moment, with a focus on empathy and authenticity. It involves taking a step back from the chaos of daily life and making time for self-care, reflection, and emotional intelligence. This approach can lead to a range of benefits, including:

Reduced Stress and Anxiety

Mindful leadership encourages individuals to take a more holistic approach to their lives, including their work. By taking time to reflect and focus on self-care, individuals can reduce stress and anxiety levels, which in turn can help them become more productive and focused.

Improved Decision-Making

Mindful leaders are better equipped to make sound decisions because they take the time to analyze situations, consider multiple perspectives and weigh the pros and cons before taking action. This approach helps to reduce impulsive decisions, which can lead to unforeseen consequences.

Enhanced Creativity and Innovation

Mindful leaders encourage creativity and innovation by creating a safe space for employees to share their ideas and perspectives. This approach fosters trust and collaboration, which can lead to new ideas and breakthroughs.

Increased Self-Awareness

Mindful leadership promotes self-awareness, which is essential for personal and professional growth. By being mindful of their own thoughts and feelings, leaders can better understand their strengths and weaknesses, and take steps to improve their performance.

Greater Empathy and Compassion

Mindful leaders are more empathetic and compassionate towards their employees, which can lead to a more positive work environment. This approach helps to build trust and loyalty among employees, which can lead to higher levels of engagement and productivity.

In conclusion, mindful leadership is not just a passing trend, but an essential practice for anyone who wants to succeed in today's business world. By taking a more holistic approach to their lives, individuals can reduce stress and anxiety levels, make better decisions, foster creativity and innovation, increase self-awareness, and cultivate greater empathy and compassion towards others. By embracing mindful leadership, women, parents, and business owners can create a more positive and productive work environment while promoting mental wellness and reducing stress.

Chapter 6: Mindfulness for Parent-Entrepreneurs
The Challenges of Juggling Parenthood and Entrepreneurship

Parenthood and entrepreneurship are two major responsibilities that demand a great deal of time, energy, and effort. As a woman, parent, and business owner, juggling both roles can be incredibly challenging. The constant demands of parenting and running a business can be overwhelming, leaving many women feeling stressed and burnt out. In this subchapter, we will explore the challenges of juggling parenthood and entrepreneurship and provide some tips for managing stress and promoting mental wellness.

One of the main challenges of juggling parenthood and entrepreneurship is time management. It can be difficult to find the time to run a business while also caring for children. Parents often have to balance their work schedules with their children's needs, such as school drop-offs and pick-ups, extracurricular activities, and doctor's appointments. This can leave little time for running a business or taking care of oneself.

Another challenge is the emotional toll that parenting and entrepreneurship can take. Parenthood can be emotionally taxing, as parents worry about their children's well-being and struggle to balance their own needs with those of their children. Entrepreneurship can also be emotionally challenging, as business owners face the pressure of making their business a success and dealing with setbacks and failures.

To manage these challenges, it is essential to prioritize self-care and mental wellness. This means taking time for oneself, practicing stress-reducing techniques, and seeking support when needed. Some tips for managing stress and promoting mental wellness include:

1. Prioritize self-care: Make time for activities that promote mental wellness, such as exercise, meditation, and spending time in nature.

2. Set boundaries: Establish clear boundaries between work and family time to avoid burnout and ensure that both roles receive the attention they need.

3. Seek support: Reach out to family, friends, or professionals for support when needed. Having a support system can help reduce stress and provide a sense of community.

4. Practice mindfulness: Practice mindfulness techniques, such as deep breathing and visualization, to reduce stress and improve focus.

In conclusion, juggling parenthood and entrepreneurship can be incredibly challenging, but it is possible to manage the stress and promote mental wellness. By prioritizing self-care, setting boundaries, seeking support, and practicing mindfulness, women, parents, and business owners can find balance and thrive in both roles.

Techniques for Mindful Parenting and Entrepreneurship

Parenting and entrepreneurship are two of the most challenging roles that one could take on. Both require immense dedication, commitment, and hard work. However, juggling both can be a daunting task, and it can be overwhelming at times. The good news is that it is possible to balance both roles with mindfulness. Mindful parenting and entrepreneurship are all about being present in the moment and focusing on what you are doing at that particular time.

The following techniques can help you achieve mindfulness in your parenting and business life:

1. Practice self-care: As a parent and entrepreneur, it is crucial to take care of your mental and physical health. This includes eating healthy, exercising, and getting enough sleep. When you are well-rested and healthy, you can focus better on your business and family.

2. Set realistic goals: Being mindful means setting achievable goals for yourself. This includes setting specific, measurable, and realistic goals that align with your values and priorities. It is essential to break down your goals into smaller, manageable tasks that you can accomplish daily.

3. Prioritize your time: Being a parent and entrepreneur means that you have numerous responsibilities. To be mindful, you need to prioritize your time and focus on what is essential. This means setting boundaries and saying no to things that do not align with your values and priorities.

4. Practice active listening: Mindful parenting and entrepreneurship require active listening. This means giving your full attention to your children or clients when they are talking to you. It also means being present in the moment and not getting distracted by other things.

5. Practice gratitude: Being grateful for the things you have in your life is a great way to practice mindfulness. Take a few minutes each day to reflect on the things you are grateful for, and this can help you stay positive and motivated.

In conclusion, being a mindful parent and entrepreneur requires practice and dedication. By practicing self-care, setting realistic goals, prioritizing your time, practicing active listening, and practicing gratitude, you can achieve mindfulness in both areas of your life. Remember that being mindful is all about being present in the moment and focusing on what you are doing at that particular time.

The Benefits of Mindful Parent-Entrepreneurship

Parenting and entrepreneurship are two of the most challenging roles a person can take on. The combination of these two roles can be even more daunting, but it is not impossible. Mindful parent-entrepreneurship is a practice that can help parents who are also business owners to balance their personal and professional lives. This subchapter will discuss the benefits of mindful parent-entrepreneurship and how it can help women, parents, and business owners.

One of the benefits of mindful parent-entrepreneurship is that it promotes mental wellness. Mindfulness is a practice that involves focusing on the present moment without judgment. It can help entrepreneurs to manage stress, reduce anxiety, and improve their overall mental health. Mindful parenting can also help parents to be present with their children, which can improve their relationships and reduce stress within the family.

Another benefit of mindful parent-entrepreneurship is that it can help business owners to be more productive. Being mindful means focusing on one task at a time and avoiding distractions. This can help entrepreneurs to be more efficient and get more done in less time. Mindful parenting can also help parents to prioritize their time and focus on what is most important.

Mindful parent-entrepreneurship can also improve communication and relationships. Mindfulness can help entrepreneurs to be more empathetic and understanding towards their employees and customers. It can also help parents to communicate more effectively with their children and partners. This can lead to improved relationships both at home and in the workplace.

Finally, mindful parent-entrepreneurship can help entrepreneurs to find a work-life balance. This can be especially important for women who often juggle multiple roles. Being mindful can help entrepreneurs to set boundaries and prioritize their time. It can also help them to avoid burnout and achieve a better work-life balance.

In conclusion, mindful parent-entrepreneurship is a practice that can benefit women, parents, and business owners. It promotes mental wellness, improves productivity, communication, and relationships, and helps entrepreneurs to achieve a better work-life balance. By practicing mindfulness, parents can be present with their children and successful in their businesses.

Chapter 7: Mindful Self-Care for Women Entrepreneurs
The Importance of Self-Care for Women Entrepreneurs

The Importance of Self-Care for Women Entrepreneurs

As a woman entrepreneur, it is essential to prioritize your mental health and well-being. Running a business can be extremely stressful, and it is easy to get caught up in the daily grind. However, neglecting self-care can have detrimental effects on both your mental and physical health.

Self-care involves taking care of your body, mind, and soul. It means setting aside time for activities that bring you joy and relaxation, such as exercise, meditation, or spending time with loved ones. It also means recognizing when you need a break and allowing yourself to step away from work when necessary.

When women entrepreneurs prioritize self-care, they can reduce stress, increase productivity, and improve overall well-being. By taking care of their mental health, they can also better handle the challenges that come with running a business.

One way to practice self-care is to establish a routine that includes exercise, healthy eating, and sleep. Exercise has been shown to reduce stress and improve mood, while eating a healthy diet can provide the necessary nutrients for the body and mind to function at its best. Getting enough sleep is also crucial for mental and physical health.

Another effective way to practice self-care is to schedule time for activities that bring joy and relaxation. This can include anything from reading a book to taking a bubble bath. It is important to make time for these activities and prioritize them in your schedule.

Finally, it is important to recognize when you need a break and allow yourself to step away from work. Taking a day off or even just a few hours to recharge can do wonders for your mental health and well-being.

In conclusion, self-care is crucial for women entrepreneurs. It allows them to reduce stress, increase productivity, and improve overall well-being. By prioritizing self-care, women entrepreneurs can better handle the challenges that come with running a business and achieve greater success in both their personal and professional lives.

Techniques for Mindful Self-Care

As business owners and parents, we often find ourselves juggling multiple responsibilities, deadlines, and expectations. It can be easy to get caught up in the chaos of our daily lives and neglect our own well-being. However, taking care of ourselves is not only important for our own mental health, but it can also have a positive impact on our relationships, work performance, and overall quality of life.

Mindful self-care is a practice that can help us prioritize our own needs and reduce stress. Here are a few techniques that can be incorporated into daily routines to promote mental wellness:

1. Mindful breathing: Taking a few deep breaths and focusing on the present moment can help calm the mind and reduce anxiety. This technique can be done anywhere, anytime, and can be especially helpful during stressful situations.

2. Gratitude journaling: Taking a few minutes each day to write down things we are grateful for can help shift our focus to the positive aspects of our lives. This technique can help us appreciate what we have and reduce feelings of stress and overwhelm.

3. Mindful movement: Engaging in physical activity such as yoga, stretching, or walking can help reduce stress and improve mood. Mindful movement involves focusing on the sensations of the body and being present in the moment.

4. Self-compassion: Practicing self-compassion involves treating ourselves with the same kindness and understanding that we would offer to a friend. This technique can help reduce self-criticism and improve self-esteem.

5. Mindful eating: Paying attention to the taste, texture, and smell of food can help us enjoy the experience of eating and reduce stress. This technique involves being present and mindful during meals, rather than eating on autopilot.

Incorporating these techniques into our daily routines can help promote mental wellness and reduce stress. As business owners and parents, it is important to prioritize our own well-being in order to better serve those around us. Mindful self-care is a powerful tool that can help us do just that.

The Benefits of Mindful Self-Care

The Benefits of Mindful Self-Care

As an entrepreneur, taking care of yourself is essential to achieving success. However, many business owners neglect their own needs, putting their mental and physical health at risk. Mindful self-care is a practice that focuses on taking care of oneself, both mentally and physically. Here are some benefits of practicing mindful self-care:

Reduced Stress

Stress is a common issue for entrepreneurs. However, when it becomes chronic, it can have a negative impact on your mental and physical health. Mindful self-care techniques, such as meditation, deep breathing, and yoga, can help reduce stress levels and promote relaxation.

Improved Mental Health

Mental health is just as important as physical health. Mindful self-care techniques can help improve mental health by reducing anxiety, depression, and other mental health conditions. Taking time to focus on yourself can help you become more aware of your thoughts and emotions, which can help you manage them better.

Increased Productivity

Taking time to care for yourself can actually increase your productivity. When you take a break to practice mindfulness, you clear your mind and reduce stress levels. This can help you focus better and be more productive when you return to work.

Better Relationships

Mindful self-care can also improve your relationships. When you take care of yourself, you are better able to take care of others. Practicing mindfulness can help you become more present and attentive, which can improve your relationships with family, friends, and colleagues.

Improved Physical Health

Taking care of yourself also means taking care of your physical health. Mindful self-care techniques, such as exercise, healthy eating, and getting enough sleep, can improve your physical health and help you feel better overall.

In conclusion, practicing mindful self-care is essential for entrepreneurs. It can help reduce stress levels, improve mental health, increase productivity, improve relationships, and improve physical health. Taking care of yourself is not selfish, it is necessary for achieving success in business and in life.

Chapter 8: Mindful Entrepreneurship for Mental Wellness
The Connection Between Entrepreneurship and Mental Wellness

The Connection Between Entrepreneurship and Mental Wellness

Entrepreneurship can be a thrilling and rewarding experience, but it also comes with its fair share of challenges. From managing finances to dealing with employees, entrepreneurs are constantly under pressure to make difficult decisions. This can take a toll on their mental health and wellbeing. As a result, it's important for entrepreneurs to prioritize their mental wellness to ensure they are able to run their businesses effectively.

In recent years, there has been a growing awareness of the connection between entrepreneurship and mental wellness. Studies have shown that entrepreneurs are more likely to experience mental health issues such as depression, anxiety, and burnout. This is due in part to the stress and uncertainty that comes with running a business. However, there are also factors such as isolation, financial pressure, and the constant need to innovate that can contribute to poor mental health.

Women, parents and business owners are particularly vulnerable to these challenges. Women entrepreneurs often have to juggle multiple roles and responsibilities, both at work and at home. Parents who run their own businesses may struggle to find a work-life balance, leading to feelings of guilt and overwhelm. Meanwhile, small business owners may feel isolated and unsupported, especially if they are working alone or with a small team.

The good news is that there are steps entrepreneurs can take to promote their mental wellness and reduce stress. Mindfulness and self-care practices can be particularly effective in helping entrepreneurs manage their mental health. Techniques such as meditation, yoga, and deep breathing can help entrepreneurs reduce stress and anxiety, while also improving their focus and concentration.

Other strategies that can promote mental wellness include setting boundaries, prioritizing self-care, and seeking support from others. Entrepreneurs may also benefit from seeking professional help when needed, such as therapy or counseling.

In conclusion, entrepreneurs need to prioritize their mental wellness in order to run successful businesses. By practicing mindfulness and self-care, setting boundaries, and seeking support when needed, entrepreneurs can reduce stress and promote mental wellness. This is especially important for women, parents, and small business owners who may be particularly vulnerable to the challenges of entrepreneurship.

Techniques for Mindful Entrepreneurship

As an entrepreneur, it can be easy to get caught up in the daily grind of running a business. The pressures of meeting deadlines, securing funding, and managing a team can take a toll on your mental health. However, practicing mindfulness can help you remain calm, focused, and productive. Here are some techniques for mindful entrepreneurship.

1. Start your day with meditation or mindfulness practices.

Before diving into your workday, take a few moments to center yourself. You can try meditation, deep breathing exercises, or a mindfulness practice like yoga. This will help you set a positive tone for the day and reduce stress.

2. Take regular breaks throughout the day.

Sitting at a desk for hours on end can be physically and mentally exhausting. Take regular breaks to stretch, walk around, or do something that brings you joy. This will help you stay energized and focused throughout the day.

3. Practice gratitude.

It's easy to get caught up in the challenges of running a business, but taking time to appreciate what you have can help reduce stress and promote mental wellness. Write down three things you're grateful for each day, whether it's a supportive team member, a successful project, or a personal accomplishment.

4. Set realistic goals and prioritize.

As an entrepreneur, it's important to set realistic goals and prioritize your tasks to avoid feeling overwhelmed. Take a few moments each day to assess what needs to be done and what can wait.

5. Practice self-compassion.

Entrepreneurship can be challenging, and it's important to be kind to yourself when things don't go as planned. Instead of beating yourself up over a mistake, practice self-compassion and remind yourself that everyone makes mistakes.

By incorporating these techniques into your daily routine, you can promote mental wellness and reduce stress as an entrepreneur. Remember to prioritize your mental health and well-being, as they are crucial to your success as a business owner.

The Benefits of Mindful Entrepreneurship

The Benefits of Mindful Entrepreneurship

As a woman, parent, or business owner, it's easy to get caught up in the fast-paced nature of entrepreneurship. The never-ending to-do lists, deadlines, and the constant pressure to perform can lead to stress, anxiety, and burnout. However, there's a solution to this problem - mindful entrepreneurship.

Mindful entrepreneurship involves using mindfulness techniques to reduce stress, promote mental wellness, and improve overall business performance. Here are some of the benefits of practicing mindful entrepreneurship:

1. Reduced Stress and Anxiety

One of the most significant benefits of mindful entrepreneurship is that it helps to reduce stress and anxiety. Mindfulness techniques such as meditation, deep breathing, and yoga can help to calm the mind, reduce stress levels, and improve overall mental wellbeing. As a result, entrepreneurs can make better decisions, be more productive, and achieve their goals more effectively.

2. Improved Productivity

Mindful entrepreneurship can help to improve productivity by helping entrepreneurs to focus their attention on the task at hand. By practicing mindfulness techniques, entrepreneurs can become more present in the moment, avoid distractions, and complete tasks more efficiently. This increased productivity can lead to improved business performance and increased profitability.

3. Enhanced Creativity

Mindful entrepreneurship can also enhance creativity by promoting a more relaxed and open mindset. When entrepreneurs are less stressed and more relaxed, they are better able to tap into their creative potential and come up with innovative ideas. This enhanced creativity can lead to new business opportunities, increased revenue, and improved overall business success.

4. Improved Health and Wellbeing

Finally, mindful entrepreneurship can also lead to improved health and wellbeing. By reducing stress levels and promoting mental wellness, entrepreneurs can improve their physical health, reduce the risk of burnout, and enjoy a higher quality of life. This improved health and wellbeing can also lead to improved business success, as healthy and happy entrepreneurs are more likely to achieve their goals and make better decisions.

In conclusion, mindful entrepreneurship is an essential practice for women, parents, and business owners who are looking to promote mental wellness, reduce stress, and improve overall business performance. By practicing mindfulness techniques, entrepreneurs can enjoy a range of benefits, including reduced stress and anxiety, improved productivity, enhanced creativity, and improved health and wellbeing. So, if you're looking to achieve success while maintaining a healthy work-life balance, consider incorporating mindful entrepreneurship into your daily routine.

Chapter 9: The Future of Mindful Entrepreneurship
The Growth of Mindful Entrepreneurship

The Growth of Mindful Entrepreneurship

In recent years, the business world has experienced a shift towards a more mindful approach to entrepreneurship. Mindful entrepreneurship is the practice of running a business with a focus on both profitability and the well-being of employees, customers, and the community. This approach emphasizes the importance of self-care, mental wellness, and ethical business practices.

Women, parents, and business owners are increasingly seeking ways to balance their personal and professional lives while prioritizing their mental health. Mindful entrepreneurship provides a framework for achieving this balance by promoting self-awareness, compassion, and mindfulness in the workplace.

One of the key tenets of mindful entrepreneurship is the practice of self-care. This involves taking care of oneself physically, mentally, and emotionally. Women, parents, and business owners can benefit from incorporating practices such as meditation, yoga, and exercise into their daily routines. These practices promote mental wellness, reduce stress, and increase productivity.

Another important aspect of mindful entrepreneurship is ethical business practices. This involves making decisions that consider the impact on all stakeholders, including employees, customers, and the environment. Women, parents, and business owners can benefit from incorporating sustainable and socially responsible practices into their businesses. These practices not only benefit the community but also contribute to the long-term success of the business.

In addition to self-care and ethical business practices, mindful entrepreneurship also emphasizes the importance of mindfulness in the workplace. Mindfulness involves being present in the moment and being aware of one's thoughts and emotions. This practice can improve focus, reduce stress, and increase creativity. Women, parents, and business owners can benefit from incorporating mindfulness practices such as meditation and breathing exercises into their daily routines.

The growth of mindful entrepreneurship reflects a shift towards a more holistic approach to business. Women, parents, and business owners can benefit from incorporating these practices into their businesses to promote mental wellness, reduce stress, and achieve success. By prioritizing self-care, ethical business practices, and mindfulness, entrepreneurs can create a workplace that is not only profitable but also promotes well-being for all stakeholders.

The Role of Mindful Entrepreneurship in Business

The Role of Mindful Entrepreneurship in Business

In today's fast-paced and competitive business world, entrepreneurs often find themselves struggling to keep up with the demands of running a successful enterprise. The pressure to perform can take a toll on their mental health and wellbeing, leading to stress, anxiety, and burnout.

This is where mindful entrepreneurship comes in. Mindful entrepreneurship is the practice of applying mindfulness techniques to the business world, allowing entrepreneurs to reduce stress, increase productivity, and promote mental wellness.

The benefits of mindful entrepreneurship are numerous. By practicing mindfulness, entrepreneurs can learn to focus on the present moment, rather than getting caught up in worries about the future or regrets about the past. This can lead to increased clarity of thought, better decision-making, and improved overall performance.

Mindful entrepreneurship also helps entrepreneurs to manage stress and anxiety. By practicing mindfulness techniques such as meditation, breathing exercises, and yoga, entrepreneurs can learn to calm their minds and reduce the negative impact of stress on their bodies and minds.

In addition to promoting mental wellness, mindful entrepreneurship can also lead to a more fulfilling business experience. By focusing on the present moment and being mindful of their surroundings, entrepreneurs can develop a deeper appreciation for their work and the people around them. This can lead to increased satisfaction and a sense of purpose in their work.

For women and parents who are entrepreneurs, mindful entrepreneurship can be especially beneficial. Women and parents often face unique challenges in the business world, such as managing work-life balance and dealing with societal expectations. Mindful entrepreneurship can help them to navigate these challenges with greater ease and resilience.

In conclusion, the role of mindful entrepreneurship in business cannot be overstated. By practicing mindfulness techniques, entrepreneurs can reduce stress, increase productivity, and promote mental wellness. For women, parents, and business owners in particular, mindful entrepreneurship can be a powerful tool for achieving success and fulfillment in their work and personal lives.

The Potential of Mindful Entrepreneurship for Mental Wellness

Mindful entrepreneurship is a relatively new concept that has emerged in recent years. It combines the principles of mindfulness with the tenets of entrepreneurship to create a holistic approach to business that promotes mental wellness and reduces stress. The potential of mindful entrepreneurship for mental wellness is significant, and it offers many benefits for women, parents, and business owners who are looking to prioritize their mental health self-care.

The first benefit of mindful entrepreneurship is that it promotes self-awareness. By practicing mindfulness, entrepreneurs can become more attuned to their thoughts and emotions, which can help them identify and manage stressors more effectively. This increased self-awareness can also help entrepreneurs make better decisions, as they are more in tune with their intuition and can tap into their creativity more easily.

Another benefit of mindful entrepreneurship is that it promotes resilience. Entrepreneurship can be a challenging and stressful journey, and it is natural to experience setbacks and failures along the way. However, by practicing mindfulness, entrepreneurs can develop the resilience needed to bounce back from these challenges and keep moving forward. This resilience can also help entrepreneurs stay focused on their goals and maintain their motivation, even in the face of adversity.

Mindful entrepreneurship also promotes a sense of purpose and meaning. When entrepreneurs are mindful, they are more in tune with their values and their mission, which can help them stay connected to their purpose and drive. This sense of purpose can be especially important for women and parents, who may be juggling multiple roles and responsibilities. By staying connected to their purpose, entrepreneurs can stay focused on what matters most and avoid getting overwhelmed by the day-to-day demands of running a business.

In summary, mindful entrepreneurship has significant potential for promoting mental wellness and reducing stress. By practicing mindfulness, entrepreneurs can develop self-awareness, resilience, and a sense of purpose and meaning, all of which are essential for maintaining mental wellness in the face of the challenges of entrepreneurship. For women, parents, and business owners who are looking to prioritize their mental health self-care, mindful entrepreneurship is a powerful tool that can help them achieve their goals and stay focused on what matters most.

Conclusion: The Power of Mindful Entrepreneurship for Mental Wellness

In conclusion, the power of mindful entrepreneurship for mental wellness cannot be overstated. Mindfulness techniques and practices can help you reduce stress, increase focus, and improve your overall well-being. In today's fast-paced business world, it's more important than ever to take care of your mental health.

As women and parents, we often juggle multiple responsibilities and face unique challenges in our careers. It can be easy to become overwhelmed and stressed out. However, by incorporating mindfulness into our daily routines, we can learn to manage our stress levels and maintain a healthy work-life balance.

Entrepreneurs, in particular, face high levels of stress and uncertainty. Mindfulness can help you cope with these challenges and stay focused on your goals. By practicing mindfulness techniques such as meditation and deep breathing, you can improve your mental clarity and creative thinking abilities.

As business owners, it's important to prioritize mental wellness in the workplace. By creating a supportive and positive work environment, you can help your employees manage their stress levels and improve their overall well-being. Encouraging mindfulness practices such as yoga and meditation can also have a positive impact on employee productivity and morale.

In this book, we've explored a variety of mindfulness techniques and practices that can help you reduce stress and promote mental wellness in your business. From meditation and deep breathing to yoga and mindfulness-based stress reduction, there are many ways to incorporate mindfulness into your daily routine.

In conclusion, the power of mindful entrepreneurship for mental wellness is undeniable. By incorporating mindfulness practices into your daily routine, you can reduce stress, increase focus, and improve your overall well-being. As women, parents, and business owners, it's important to prioritize mental health and well-being in all aspects of our lives.